HOW TO MAKE MONEY

By J.D. Thornton

SCHOLASTIC INC.
New York Toronto London Auckland Sydney
Mexico City New Delhi Hong Kong Buenos Aires

PROPERTY OF:

_____

ISBN-13: 978-0-545-07195-6
ISBN-10: 0-545-07195-X

12 11 10 9 8 7 6 5 4 3 2 1   8 9 10 11 12 13/0

Printed in the U.S.A.   40

This edition first printing, February 2008

Text by J.D. Thornton
Graphic design by Stewart Yule
Cover by Tammy Shafer
Typeset in New Century Schoolbook

Contents

HOW TO MAKE MONEY

Ka-ching, Ka-ching!

Aren't you sick and tired of having to beg and plead every time you want a little more than just lunch money? Bet your folks are! Well, guess what? It doesn't have to be that way! You're never too young to start taking charge and earning your own money! And, no, we're not talkin' petty cash—we're talkin' some serious 'ching 'ching for your bling bling! Your pockets will soon be so fat that you'll have to buy yourself bigger pants!

How to Make Money is the ultimate guide to get you proactive, creative and, of course, some money! Whether you want more dough to buy a new set of wheels, the latest sneakers, a gift for a special friend, or to save for a rainy day (you know, in case you need to buy an umbrella) you'll soon see that the money-making opportunities are absolutely everywhere!

Inside you'll find awesome tips on getting started and tapping into your skills to come up with ideas on fun stuff you can make and sell, the kinds of services you can provide, effective ways of selling and promoting your product, plus fantastic advice on how to manage your money. You can even scribble down your ideas as you read along on the "your ideas" pages that you will find throughout.

Like to cook? Have a cake sale! Good with animals? Offer your dog-walking services! Yeah, it's true money doesn't grow on trees (darn!), but your gardening skills could grow a cash crop! You could even brainstorm with friends, consider your collective skills and then draw up a plan to save for a super-fun big day out, or for your favorite charity—whatever YOU want!

And just imagine how fantastic and rewarding it will feel to have fresh cash in your fingers knowing that YOU earned every last cent!

So get proactive, be your own boss and make your own money so that you can determine what's yours and when. What are you waiting for? Time is money! Quit crossing your fingers and waiting around for Christmas! Read on and let the ideas, action and buck bonanza begin!

Chapter 1

GETTING STARTED

What are you good at and what do you love to do?!

If you know what you're good at and what you love to do then starting should be easy. If you're not sure, then spend some time researching—that is, asking questions to find out what people in your neighborhood and local community are either buying or needing done, that you can sell or do.

For example if you love working with clay, you can

make some garden pots in all sorts of shapes and sizes, then paint them in bright colors. You may even grow some herbs to put in them and sell to the local flower shop or at your next school event. Or, if you're clever at fixing things, you can buy an old, dinged skateboard and restore it by re-shaping it, adding a snazzy new design and re-oiling the ball bearings to make the wheels run smoother.

Brainstorm some money-making ideas with your family and with good planning and organizing it will be easy for you to make money doing either what you love or whatever needs doing! You may even find some new things that you have never tried before that you will also really enjoy.

Researching

It always pays to do some research before you start. Your parents, family, books and the internet are good ways to get more info to help you do a better job. Remember, the more questions you ask, the more you will learn.

Organizing

It pays (literally) to plan
ahead so that you're
well organized. If you do
this well, by planning
before action, then you
won't waste time or get
frustrated. The more time
you spend doing something,
the more it's actually
costing you . . . so the trick is

to be economical and plan well. Try planning on large
pieces of paper so you can easily see what needs doing
or make a TO DO list with due dates for each activity.

Keeping records

Keeping a record of what you spend, what you earn
and time spent is important so that you know you are
making money and not losing it. We have created a
Record-keeping Book with some basic records in the
back of the book to get you started.

Win-win!

A simple rule to keep in mind is called Win–win,
which means that if you win and the buyer and seller
also win, then it's a great deal. You may have to
compromise a little to achieve this. Winning isn't about
getting something totally your own way.

Warnings!

Personal safety is of the utmost importance and most of the activities in this book will benefit from some adult supervision or input. We recommend that you discuss with an adult what you are going to do so that they can help. We stress that any activity that may involve dealing with strangers should *always* be supervised by a parent or guardian.

The Law

Images that are marked with a copyright line and/or the symbol © belong to other people, so you are not allowed to re-use them to resell unless you get the owner's permission. If you do use it with their permission, they may charge you a percentage of your sale price. If you use it without their permission, you are breaking the law.

Keep in mind also that anything original that you create can have your copyright on it. Simply write small somewhere on the back and bottom of your creation: © [Year], [Your Name].

Q: What do you get if you cross a sorceress with a billionaire?
A: A very witch person.

My Goals

List or draw your money-making goals!

NOW!—Short-Term Goals

_____

_____

_____

_____

_____

LATER!—Long-Term Goals

_____

_____

_____

_____

_____

My Top 10

Things to save for!

_____

_____

_____

_____

_____

_____

_____

_____

_____

_____

_____

_____

_____

Chapter 2

Stuff You Can Sell to Make Money (Goods)

Here's an alphabetical list of things that you can make, buy second-hand, collect or grow. What appeals to you will probably depend on your natural skills. Always be creative and try something even if you don't know how it will go—you never know until you have a try!

TOP TIP!

**Once you've worked out what you want to do most,
create a flyer (see Marketing Materials in Chapter 4)
and pass it around, and even do mailbox drops on
your street (if your parents are OK with that).**

Make

It's fun to make original things, as well as things out
of all sorts of stuff, but remember not to use images
(or in some cases things) that belong to other people
who own the copyright. See the section on The Law
in Chapter 1. You can either take the fully handmade
craft approach or utilize your computer to create the
designs. Try out a few samples first to see what people
like most. If you do this well your designs will be
popular and make money. Be inspired by what others
have done but try to be a little (or a lot) different in
everything you do; then you will stand out.

Cooking

We know ALL kids love eating baked yummies and
there's a lot of you out there who also love to bake
cakes, cookies, tarts, brownies . . . the list goes on.
Whatever takes your fancy! Depending on your skills
you may need some adult supervision. You will also

TOP TIP!

Remember to keep your work as neat and clean as possible (even seal the finished item to protect it if appropriate). The more professional they look, the more you can charge, the more you will sell and—the best bit—the more money you will make for your efforts!

need some assistance in purchasing the ingredients. It will help to know where you are going to sell them (maybe at your school party), and how many you are going to bake. Some things freeze OK for another time but it's always better to sell "freshly baked" goods.

Beauty products

You can find some great organic recipes in books, mags or on the internet for all sorts of products such as exfoliates, hand creams, face cleansers, even blended oils for burning, and then you can make up your own range from the best ingredients. Test as you go to make sure people like them and that they are suitable for sensitive skins. Then make some little labels with a catchy name to go on the containers. Don't forget to list the ingredients and say it's organic, which is a great selling point.

Calendars

Calendars are sold from September onwards for the following year. They can be a 12- or perhaps a 16-month calendar. Copy the layout of an old calendar, making sure to get the dates right for the next year. Use prints of photos you've taken or create a special design for each month. You could help Mom out (for a price, of course) for Gran's birthday and do a personalized calendar, and you can use your own family photos.

Making things with clay

If you're good with your hands and like to make things then this could suit you. You can buy clay from a craft or art store. Fimo, a finer clay, is ideal for making jewelry and comes in a large range of colors. You can make little pots for herbs, ring stands or even miniature animals.

Q: Why did the nun walk around with her purse open?
A: She'd read there was going to be some change in the weather.

TOP TIP!

Remember anything goes as long as you can sell it. Sometimes it will be trial and error before your creations are good enough and you find designs that buyers like. Craft shops are great for inspiration and may also have books with modeling techniques. Spend some time looking around and you will no doubt end up with more ideas than you went in with.

Craft ideas

If you have a knack for using your hands, are deft with
a glue gun and love sprucing things up, then these
super crafty ideas will get you started. Remember to
put newspaper down first and keep a neat workspace.
Be patient for things to dry and always clean up after
yourself (even if you have your own workspace)!

$ Bags – Any old bag can be funked up with a bit of
imagination, so be as creative as you want. As long as
it is appealing you should be able to sell it. Sell one
with a discount to your big sister and make sure she
tells everyone where she got it!

$ Book covers – Using anything from denim to fur
fabric looks cool. Remember the cover needs to be a little
bit bigger than the book and will need folds sealed on the
edges to slip the book into. Ask an adult for help here.

$ Funking up old clothes – Either sew or paint a
design using fabric paint. Remember, most supplies
can be bought at a craft store or even at a discount shop.

$ Hats – To a new, plain hat, or even tired old hats, add
ribbons, feathers, brooches or flowers, or a mix of all!

$ Journals – Make new covers or stick designs straight

**Q: What happened when the cat
swallowed a coin?
A: There was money in the kitty.**

onto existing cover. You could also add a tie-on pen.

Ⓢ Knitting – Find some basic knitting patterns for doll's clothes, baby booties or small animals such as teddy bears.

Ⓢ Photo frames – Spruce up dull old frames with shells and beads.

Ⓢ Sewing – Some kids learn to sew on a machine but if that's not you then you can always use just the good ol' needle and thread (and a thimble of course!) to fix or make anything that inspires you.

TOP TIP!

Create a Craft Box. Collect buttons, needles
and threads, scissors, glue gun, bits of ribbon and lace
and anything else that looks like it can be used to
dress something up. The more you have at your
disposal the more creative you can be.

TOP TIP!

Make your own presents and save money this
Christmas. Earning is important but so is saving!
If you are 12+ you can offer to buy others' gifts if they
are too busy. Make sure you get a detailed list, the
cash and price range before you set out and make sure
you can return the items in case they aren't right.

Christmas gifts

We all know how expensive
Christmas can be and
people are always looking
for ways to save. Here
are some ideas for you to
explore:

⑤ Cards – Work out one
great design, make heaps of
Christmas cards and include
small tag-type ones that
can be used on presents.
Box them in 5s or 10s or sell
them separately.

⑤ Wrapping – Offer to
gift-wrap presents for family
and friends using either

their wrapping and ribbon or yours. Of course, charge more for using yours. You could make up a couple of samples so your customers can choose their preferred styles.

⑨ Bagged lollipops – Buy large assortments of lollipops from a wholesaler (ask an adult to help you find one) and find (or make) a good selection of bags or small boxes and ribbon. Mix the lollipops and fill the bags or boxes. You could also attach a small blank gift card. Make sure you keep them cool as heat will melt any chocolate or make the lollipops clump together. Don't forget to keep a record of your time to add to your costs so it can help you work out a fair price to charge.

⑨ Table decorations – A Christmas lunch or dinner table setting isn't finished without a central decoration. You can make these up out of old decorations, or out of bric-a-brac, or even paint pinecones and put them into ribboned baskets.

TOP TIP!
Make small single-sided gift cards with a simple, effective message and/or design. If you make many of the same design you can save time but still charge the same amount for each.

Q: What's the easiest way to double your money?
A: Fold it in half.

Gift cards

You can design these to be general or for special occasions such as birthdays, but the less specific they are the easier they will be to sell. You can put messages inside but a lot of cards these days are blank so they can be personalized by the card giver. You can make these up from scratch by drawing or painting your design on cardstock, using stamps, or pasting some pictures on to make a montage. You can also make 3D cards using all kinds of bits and pieces; the ideas are limited only by your imagination. Remember, cards are sold with envelopes so they will need to fit whatever size envelopes you make, have or buy to put with them.

Glass painting

You can buy cheap glass vases and glass paint from a $1 shop or from a craft shop. Plan some simple designs that you can paint and repeat on different things. Remember, keep it simple.

Paintings

If you have a talent for painting and/or drawing
why not sell your pictures, framed or unframed? The
smaller the sizes, the more you can do but the less
you can charge. It's good to have a range of prices for
buyers to choose from.

Photo album (personalized)

Create a complete photo album for someone's special
occasion. Make a mock album so you can show your
customers what you can do. Use a different family
member for every page, celebrating an event or
occasion using cut-outs and decorations. Be as creative
as you want, and try to show a few different styles.

BUY SECOND-HAND

Garage sales, thrift shops, Gran's attic!

As the saying goes, one person's trash is another's
treasure, and if you can work out which is which then
you can make money from spotting a bargain. Remember,
the cheaper you can get things for, the more money you
can make, and if you get things for free . . . even better!

Clothes

If you've got a good eye for spotting popular brands
and styles, you can make good money reselling items.
Make sure the clothes are in reasonable condition;

if they're only a bit dirty you can always wash them. It's always good to wash them anyway, because often they've been sitting in bags for a while. You might like to try making a shirt, a dress, a top, a skirt or a jacket super-funky by sewing on buttons or badges or anything that is trendy.

TOP TIP!

An adult's assistance will be not only most useful as you go about collecting things, but also advisable. Find yourself some kind of shopping bag, wheeled suitcase or cart that you can put your goods into and which can also easily be loaded into the trunk of a car.

TOP TIP!

Look in fashion magazines for ideas. If your clothes are mostly for teens then look in the teen mags too.

Bikes

Often second-hand bikes have been left out in the weather and if not too badly rusted can be polished up to look nearly new. Depending on how good you are at adjusting gears and brakes you may want to put it in for a professional service and add that cost to your sale price. And don't forget—a good clean can do wonders.

Books

Some books are more popular than others . . . and there will always be boxes of them to be found. The trick is to know which are good, although if they are being sold cheaply enough you might just take the lot and sort them out later. Re-sell some to a second-hand book store and some at your own garage sale, and maybe donate the rest that are too old or unpopular.

Bric-a-brac

Bric-a-brac is the term for all sorts of smallish things

. . . in the garage-sale world anyway. Sometimes these things just need a bit of paint, a good clean, or a dab of glue. Often people can't be bothered doing these things so they throw them out, but if you can, you can benefit.

Furniture

Unless you have an adult helping, large pieces such as beds and wardrobes will be impractical, but stools and little tables and chairs are light enough and easier to spruce up with a bit of paint or polish.

Records

Before CDs there were vinyl records—albums, EPs and singles. Depending on the quality and rarity these can be good resellers. There are second-hand stores that will buy these if they are in good condition.

Q: Where do pigs put their money?
A: In a piggy bank.

Trimmings

Trimmings are the name for stuff such as buttons, ribbon, lace, patches, beads and anything else that you can add to something to "spruce" it up. You can resell by bundling them into little craft bags, or collect for yourself so you've always got things on hand when you need to express your creativity on some dull old thing!

GROW

If you've got a bit of a "green thumb" (meaning good at growing things and not killing them!) and you enjoy seeing the fruits of your labors, then this may be just your forté. If you need help, there's sure to be another green thumb in the family somewhere, or look up a resource book or on the internet for more info. Here are some things you can grow.

Herbs

Herbs are used for cooking many styles of food, from Italian to Indian. You can grow herbs from seeds, seedlings or small plants. The best size to sell them at will depend on the particular herb.

Flowers

Everyone loves a bunch of flowers

but you have to wait for them to grow and they can be quite difficult to keep healthy, so make sure you do your research first. Start small and maybe sell small, potted flowers first, grown from seeds or seedlings.

Fruit and veggies

If you have fruit trees in your backyard gather the fallen fruit and pick the ripe ones so you can bag them up to sell. You might even like to make some jam out of them. Veggies can be grown from pots or in a specially prepared garden. If you haven't done this before have an adult  help you work out what you need to do. If you want to start small, grow your veggies in pots (also from seeds or seedlings), where you can move them around if need be to find the best spot. It's also easier to keep bugs and grubs off them.

TOP TIP!

Make sure you have the right bug repellent for your edible plants otherwise the snails will feast nicely—but your customers won't!

Plants

You can grow bigger plants from smaller plants or even from cuttings. A lot of plants will do what is called striking, that is, the cutting will grow new roots in water. Experiment with a few plant cuttings from the garden, but check with your folks first. Once they have established a fair cluster of roots you can transfer the cutting to soil and *voila*—a new plant!

TOP TIP!
The cutting needs to include enough of a branch that has growth sprouts on it, otherwise it may not strike.

At Christmas time you could sell small, potted, live Christmas trees, and market them as: "One tree for the rest of your life! It will grow up with your kids!"

Useful tips and info

When you're out and about always keep an eye out for ideas. See what other people are doing. Keep a notebook with you and jot your thoughts down so you don't forget. If you have a camera you can even take photos for later reference. And remember, the more you do something the better you will get at it.

My Ideas

List or draw any new and inspired ideas!

_____

_____

_____

_____

_____

_____

_____

_____

_____

_____

_____

_____

My Ideas

List or draw any new and inspired ideas!

_____

_____

_____

_____

_____

_____

_____

_____

_____

_____

_____

Chapter 3

Making Money from Your Skills (Services)

Some of us are better at *doing* things for others than we are at *selling* things. Following is a list of ideas to get you started. The key is to look for a need, then fill it. For example, your mom may always run out of time to weed the garden, or your dad may complain about always washing the car after a week of having kids in it, or your grandma may need errands run. Whatever you see around you will give you ideas as to what services you can offer. Depending on your age, you may stay focused on things around the house or for close family. If your parents are comfortable with the idea, you may extend your services to your neighbors and friends. Either way, discuss the best options with your folks, set up a weekly timetable and get going!

TOP TIP! $$

Once you've worked out what you want to do most, create a flyer (try out your design on page 46) and pass it around, and even do a mailbox drop on your street (if your folks are OK with that).

Acting/modeling

If you have an outgoing personality, this may be just the thing for you—lots of fun and a neat way to earn money. Actors and models require an agent to book the work for them. They will charge a percentage (usually between 10 and 20%) to manage this work for you, including negotiating pay and contracts. To get an agent you will need to make an appointment. You will also need photos of yourself. It's advisable to get your parents to contact various reputable agents and ask if they are taking anyone on, and what they require you to do in order to meet you and then maybe represent you. Once you have this information you can provide what they need—not what you think they need. You can research various agents around town by checking the phone-book listings as well as asking anybody you know who has an agent. You may also like to join a drama group so you can learn how to be an actor, or enrol in a modeling school to learn how to be a model.

TOP TIP!

Singing and dancing are also excellent skills to have in the entertainment industry, so if you have some talent for either or both, take some lessons.

Animals

If you have a good way with animals you might want to consider dog-walking (if you don't mind picking up poop in a plastic bag!) or feeding cats when neighbors are away. You can also add other things such as plant-watering and mail-clearing to your services. To do this you will need to ask questions (and always write the TO DO list down so you don't forget) about the animals' special needs, such as what commands they respond to and where they can run off the leash. If you're not so keen on animals avoid this one as it requires an affinity and love for them to do the job well, and it's a big responsibility.

At home

There are all sorts of things you can do at home to make money, from raking the leaves to cleaning the car. Have a chat with your folks about chores that might need doing. Create a list of ideas yourself and if you focus on things that will make your family members' lives easier, the more likely they are to pay you for them! (See "Fixing things.")

Beauty

Everyone loves to be pampered! There's quite a range
of services that you can offer if you have a penchant
for grooming: washing, coloring and styling hair for a
special occasion—don't forget you can also use clips and
flowers to jazz up a hairstyle. If you have a steady hand
you can do manicures and apply nail polish. You can
do facials with the customer's own products, or yours.
Or even offer hand and foot massages—soak either in
warm, soapy water first to relax and clean them.

TOP TIP!

**Always ask your client exactly what they would like
when they book so you can be prepared for the session.
And be as professional and hygienic as possible.**

Cleaning and tidying

This can be the most unpopular activity, especially if,
like a lot of kids, you have a messy room and always
get told to clean it up. Now you may not be able to
charge money to clean something that is not only yours
but also your job to do anyway, BUT you can charge
to clean others' bedrooms, dust, wash windows and
clear cobwebs. Anything that gets dirty can be cleaned:
the garage, the bird cage, the bathroom, the windows,

the fridge and the toilet! Shoes, outdoor areas and
furniture, the car, the lawn mower—the list goes on . . .
look around and make a list, then start negotiating.

TOP TIP!

**Remember to keep to your schedule, otherwise you
may let others down. The work offered may begin to
dwindle if you don't perform responsibly. If you can't
do something at a particular time, reschedule and
make sure whoever needs to know knows and agrees.**

Computer stuff

If you are one of those whiz-kids who knows heaps
about computers (PCs and/or Macs), this could be
a perfect way for you to make money . . . because
there are a lot of adults out there who don't know
much about computers and lack the confidence to
experiment. Depending on your skills and knowledge,
you can provide services such as software
installation, back-ups and scheduling,
de-fragging, spyware checking as well as other
general maintenance. You can even download music
(legally of course) so you can set up the customer's
iPod with all their favorite music.

TOP TIP!

Make sure you document everything you do, especially if passwords are used or changed. Record these clearly so that your client can see at a glance any information they may need. This will help in case there are problems in the future.

Delivering newspapers and flyers

Ever since newspapers have been printed there have been paperboys and girls delivering and selling papers.

It can be quite difficult to get these jobs as they are very popular. Visit your local newsagent and leave your contact details with them so that if one of the delivery kids calls in sick you might be able to get a foot in. Call back every few weeks, and they will remember you and know that you are eager. Often ad material (or as we call it, junk mail) needs to be folded with other junk mail in a particular way; you might like an adult to assist you with this part because if you get it wrong you won't have a job for long.

TOP TIP! $$

All jobs require you to be responsible and this one is no exception. It's imperative that you don't try to cut corners and miss a few here and there or put more than one paper in a mailbox, because the customers will complain if they don't get their delivery. Also, don't ignore NO JUNK MAIL stickers . . . not everyone wants it.

Entertaining

This is similar to acting/modeling (see previous) but it's a lot more flexible in that you can be more proactive rather than waiting for an agent to get you work. If you can juggle or clown, be entertaining, play an instrument, spin a diabolo, do magic tricks, sing or a combination of all then you could put together a little show and sell it as special entertainment for kids' birthday parties. Maybe you have grandparents in a home who'd love to be entertained; you could ask a fee from the management or do it as a street performer and put out a hat for coin donations. If you're good enough to perform on the streets you will have to contact your local council to obtain a street performer's licence which means you will be allowed to perform legally in certain areas.

TOP TIP!

It's always good to practice first and then show an adult your show so they can direct you and help you make it better. It's always hard to self-direct . . . even the pros have directors!

Event managing

Many times adults get so busy that they need someone to help them who will remove some of their stress, and not add to it by annoying them. So when your parents are next planning a special occasion or a party, why not offer to shadow them on the night. Before the occasion you can do lots of those little jobs, such as picking up supplies on your bike or putting up the party decorations or making the punch. You could even be a waiter for the occasion or greet the guests, marking them off as they come in. There are lots of different things you can do in the pre-planning of an occasion that you can provide as part of your "party package." Don't forget to list them on your flyer.

TOP TIP!

Make up blank name tags and put each guest's name and nickname on a tag when they arrive. It's a great way to get conversations going.

Fixing things

If you have a knack with tools, glue and are a whiz with a paintbrush then you might like to look for broken things that you can fix for people, such as a rickety gate that needs a new hinge, a squeaky door that just needs an oil, or maybe a tile that needs regluing. Look around for ideas.

You can also fix old and broken second-hand things so you can resell them. (See Chapter 2 on buying second-hand items.)

Gardening

All green thumbs, hands up! Or should that be thumbs up?! If you have a green thumb it means that you are

someone who has talent for growing things and caring
for flora, which is a big part of gardening. You can offer
to do anything from raking and weeding to trimming
edges to mowing if you're allowed to use the mower. If
not, you might get a hand-mower to do nature strips.
If your thumb is quite "green" you might like to offer
to replant potted plants into the garden or even prune
(don't do this unless you do know how!) or spread mulch
over garden beds and water the garden. Working out
what to do is mostly common sense, as most people like
a clean, fresh-looking garden with clear paths and no
weeds, but your customer will tell you exactly what they
want done (and not done, too!) in most cases.

TOP TIP!

**Boiling water poured onto weeds in pavement cracks
kills them just as well as weedkiller does—but with
no poison danger to small children and animals!
Just be careful of the hot water.**

PA (personal assistant)

A PA is a little like an event manager, but duties
are performed more as a day-to-day service. For
convenience, it is something you are more likely to do
for a family member you live with. The objective is to
make the life of your "client" easier by taking over all
sorts of odd jobs. You might take calls, run errands,
drop off or pick up things and generally be a help
during certain hours. You will need to discuss in detail
the kinds of things that need to be done and when, so
you can also work out a good fee. It requires discipline,
initiative and commitment and if you fail to do what
you promised a few times, you'll end up wasting more
time than you save, and that defeats the purpose . . .
so, don't take this one on unless you think you'll enjoy
it enough to want to please your boss.

Painting

All sorts of things need painting or repainting, from
fences and gates to doors and outdoor furniture to
patios and even old pots. So, if you have a deft hand
with a brush this may just be the thing. You will need
to have a good range of reasonable-quality brushes
in your toolbox and know how to care for them so
that they last a long time. You also will need to know
a bit about paints, such as the difference between
water-based and oil-based, enamel, indoor and outdoor,

matte, gloss, etc., as they all require different cleaners and solvents. If you don't have much knowledge in this area, get an adult to help you with each job and you can learn as you go. There are also lots of neat tricks to learn, such as how to mask an edge with tape so you don't have to paint a straight line and how to stir a big tin of paint . . . with a big stick of course! And, knowing what size brushes work best for what you're doing is key. It's also important to learn how to keep your paint strokes nice and even and not let the dribbles dry.

TOP TIP!

Use a drop-sheet under your paint area to catch all the paint drips and a hat so that your hair doesn't get splattered—and wear OLD clothes or overalls.

School/community work

You might like to introduce the concept of making money to your teacher and class at school so, as a team, you can create bigger and better ideas that may also be a lot more fun! Often the community bulletin board in your local supermarket or shopping area will have notices for services required, as may your local newspaper. Keep an eye and an ear out for things you can do to make money.

Sports events

Most sports-event support is volunteer; however, often it's a great way to meet people who may become customers in other ways. Sometimes sponsors do giveaways as a way to pay the volunteers. Think of this option as not only a networking opportunity but also a guaranteed fun day out!

Teaching/tutoring

If you're very, very good at something then you're in a great position to teach it. If your strengths are for school topics such as math or art then you can offer to help or tutor other students who need assistance. You may be great at a sport, dancing or playing an instrument. There are always people who won't know as much as you who would be willing to pay someone to teach them. If your potential students are other kids then discuss with your parents how you can best approach their parents, as they will be the ones most likely paying!

Useful tips and info

Good, clear communication is one of the most important skills when dealing with people. If you are unsure of anything, always ask questions. Always state clearly what you are going to do, and when and how much it will cost. It is advisable to put this information in writing as well and keep a copy. You could do this in a standard invoice book with carbon paper that you can buy from the office supply store.

A young high school student came running in tears to her father. "Dad, you gave me some terrible financial advice!"

"I did? What did I tell you?" he said. "You told me to put my money in that big bank, and now that big bank is in trouble."

"But that's one of the largest banks in the state," he said. "There must be some mistake."

"I don't think so," she sniffed. "The ATM screen said, *Insufficient Funds*."

My Timetable

Plan your weekly timetable here!

Monday

Tuesday

Wednesday

Thursday

Friday

Saturday

Sunday

Flyer Design

Draw a rough design for your flyer!

Chapter

Ways to Sell Your Skills and Stuff

There are all sorts of ways to sell something, be it your goods or your services, from advertising on the street to word-of-mouth spread by satisfied customers. Your goal will be to work out what will work best for you. Here are some ideas to get you started.

Marketing

Marketing is the process of selling your business

so that the world knows you exist. Big companies advertise, creating their brand awareness. If nobody knows what you have to offer then it doesn't matter how good your product is.

Here are a few questions to answer that will help you make some informed marketing decisions:

1. Who are your buyers/customers?
   Who is your market?
   Are they young or old? Male or female? Do they belong to a group?
   If they are young, then your flyer design will need to appeal to them.
2. How is your "market" best contacted?
   Advertising or personal contact?
   Do you have a network of people who can spread the word?
   Who can you ask to tell others about you?
   Word-of-mouth has always been one of the most powerful ways to sell.
3. What special qualities does your product or service offer?
   Are these what your customers need or want or value?
   If you offer freshly-cut flowers can you sell them before they begin to wilt?
4. Who are your competitors?
   How are you different?
   How can you market these benefits?

You can do this exercise with your family. They are likely to have some great ideas. If you can't answer the questions, maybe you need to ask a qualified adult for some advice. Once you have some information then you can work out the best way to act on it.

TOP TIP!

Remember that asking others (and this includes your customers and potential customers) questions about what they want or need or value will always give you better answers than guessing.

Marketing material

Marketing material is an important way of telling others about what you do. Most people like something they can refer to later on that has all the information that they will need, such as who you are, what you do/sell, where they can find it as well as how and when they can contact you. Include prices too, if that's appropriate.

Posters/flyers

Sheets that you can hand out or leave at places.

Business cards

A small card with your business name, your name
and contact details. These can be useful to hand out
anytime.

Brochures

A fold-out sheet with detailed information on what
you offer and sometimes pictures, photos and/or
illustrations.

Signs

Can be fixed to your front gate and/or a fold-out
portable one that stands up (A frame) to use where you
sell your product.

Website

If you have the ability to build one or even just create a
home page then you can put everything up here. Look
at what others do and decide what works best for you.

TOP TIP!

**Always ask for feedback as you go—then your
material will be even better.**

Creating marketing material can cost money, so if
your resources are tight then you may want to swap

with someone who can create them for you and who needs something you can offer; this is often called a "contra deal," or "quid pro quo."

Promotion

Promotion is very similar to marketing but it focuses more on special things you might do to promote yourself and your business, as opposed to the usual things you do.

You might pick a special occasion to promote a discount offer of some kind. If you mow lawns, hand out flyers at Dad's football BBQ offering 20% off. Get the idea? You may even want to launch your business, throw a party and tell everyone about what you're doing and hand out as much marketing material as you have.

TOP TIP!
Gimmicks can be a great way to attract people's attention.

Incentives

There are many ways to attract more buyers by offering incentives such as discounts. You may offer "2 for 1" or a percentage (%) slashed off the price for TODAY ONLY, or add something for FREE! Businesses do this a lot when they want to clear stock (goods) so they can put in new stock or create more cash flow (movement of money) by selling more quickly. You can also offer rewards so when a customer returns they get the discount. Be inventive with this, try different things out; be wacky to attract attention. Most times you may not make as much money but it's a great way to offer a bargain, create goodwill and build a great reputation.

TOP TIP! $$

If people remember you and like you they WILL come back for more!

Testimonials

Testimonials are statements made by happy customers praising your products or services. You can use these on any of your marketing materials. It's a great way to tell others how good you are without you having to do it all the time!

"My sister Jess is the best math tutor I've ever had, I no longer struggle in class and this term I got my first A for math!"

- Claire, Jess's sister

"Young Tim has been mowing my lawns and keeping my garden neat for the past three months, they've never looked so good! I highly recommend him."

- Jasper McNulty, neighbor

TOP TIP!

You can use part of a quote on your flyer. Pick the most flattering comment and format it like this:

"... I highly recommend him." - Jasper McNulty, neighbor

Bob: "Mom, would you like to save some money?"

Mom: "I certainly would, son. Do you have any suggestions?"

Bob: "Sure. Why not buy me a bike, then I won't wear my shoes out so fast."

My Business Card

Draw a rough design for your business card!

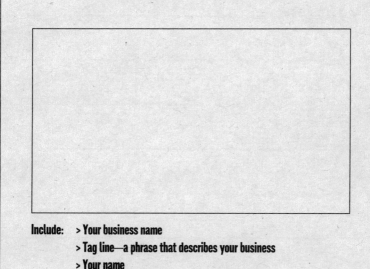

Include:
- > Your business name
- > Tag line—a phrase that describes your business
- > Your name
- > Title—are you the business owner? Manager?
- > Phone number—this is optional—ask an adult.

DAVE'S DOGWASHING

FOR CLEAN,
HAPPY DOGS!

DAVID SMITH (TOP DOG)
PHONE: 555-6541

My Ideas

List or draw any new and inspired ideas!

Chapter 5

Managing Your Money!

It's important to have plans for what to do with your money. The goal is to enjoy saving for things you want but not waste it by buying lollipops or things you won't use again. It's a good idea to put your profits or savings into a piggy bank for safekeeping, or a bank account so that it can earn interest while you save.

What is money?

mon·ey

n. pl. mon·eys or mon·ies

1. A medium that can be exchanged for goods and services and is used as a measure of their values on the market, including among its forms a commodity such as gold, an officially issued coin or note, or a deposit in a checking account or other readily liquefiable account.
2. The official currency, coins and negotiable paper notes issued by a government.

"Money makes the world go round, the world go round . . ." as the old song goes. That may not be quite the way it all works but you will find money everywhere. Money has value, which is why it's different from plain paper. In the olden days, way, way back, people traded goods or services in exchange for other goods and services that they wanted. This practice was also called bartering and some cultures still use it.

Things that were exchanged couldn't always retain their value so something was needed that could hold its value until a trader was ready to spend it. Metal pieces were first used as a form of money because they couldn't get moldy or smelly like food, although traders also used durable things such as rocks, teeth, spices, leather, pure gold and seashells to buy what they wanted. About 300 years ago paper notes were first used and now all countries of the world have currencies that come in different shapes and sizes, and have different names.

While the value of the physical money is determined by the world's stock exchanges, value is intrinsic to each person depending on what you think is valuable. Buying a great new hot-rod bike for a particular price may have great value to you but your sister may prefer a fashion doll. And so you both value different things and what your money can buy.

How to cost your time—what's it worth?

We have included a table in the back of the book so that you can keep a record of the time you spend on each project. Working out how much your time is worth can be a difficult thing and often you can't charge for the time it takes to acquire, fix, sell or do something. However, by tracking your time you may see where you spend (or waste) too much time, and where you can be more economical with how you do things, such as buying in bulk instead of one thing at a time from the most expensive place.

How to price your items to sell—what to charge

The easiest way to work out what to charge is to see what most other people charge and what most people are willing to pay for something. This will vary, so you can choose to make your prices not the most expensive and maybe not the cheapest. If your products are popular and good quality then you should be able to sell them fairly easily.

Using cash

Cash is the easiest way to get paid. If you get paid by check from a stranger (or even the odd family member) the checks might bounce (meaning they don't have enough money in the bank to pay you!) and you also have to have a bank account to put them in. Now, a bank account is a great place for saving but you may not be ready to do that, so always ask for cash—which you deposit into either a money box or a bank account. Most people won't mind, especially because you're a kid!

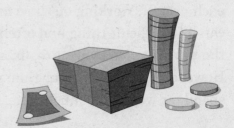

Shopping around

When you start shopping around for business or personal things that you want or need, make sure you check out more than one option. You might also find some great bargains for yourself—that skateboard might be on special for $50 instead of the RRP (recommended retail price) of $89! Some stores will lay away, which means you pay your purchase off a bit at a time over a certain period. It also means you can't spend that money on anything else!

Collecting your hard-earned cash

If you are out and about selling product at a market stall you will need somewhere safe to put your money, like a zipped waist pouch. You will also need change to give back. This is called a float. Make sure you have enough coins and bills. When you finish, you take your float back out and count your takings for the day! If you are providing a service you are likely to be paid for one job at a time, so have a wallet to keep it safe until you get home.

How to save and invest your money

To get something you really want (besides your regular birthday and Christmas presents) you will probably have to save for it, be it a new skateboard, or a new car when you're older. So, when you begin to get pocket money or earn money you need to create a savings plan. You can save by using a money box, or you can set up a bank account that earns interest (meaning the bank makes money on your money and pays you for that) and deposit your money into that. Because we often need money for more than one thing, it's useful to work out how much we need for what item. For example, you earn $20; you might put $10 away for your new bike and $5 away for some new clothes and spend $5 at the movies. Remember, if you have borrowed money you will need to put some aside to pay that back too, even if it's not the full amount.

Goals and milestones

Sometimes what we want can seem too hard to get because it's a lot of money or we don't think we can wait, or we might think it's easier to nag our parents for it instead. But if you save a bit at a time you will be amazed at how quickly it grows and before long you will have enough to buy your special thing. Sometimes parents will reward our efforts by matching our savings or adding some in. Milestones are smaller goals set along the way so that it doesn't seem like one big thing. A smaller goal is easier to reach and when joined to a whole bunch of other goals, makes one big one. If you are trying to save $100, then set your milestones at $20, $40, $60 and $80. Each time you reach a smaller milestone make sure you reward yourself with some kind of treat.

Bank accounts

You might like to open a real bank account and put your money into that. Bank accounts pay interest (a percentage nominated by the bank) on money. That means your money makes more money by staying

Q. Where do bees stash their money?
A. In a honey box.

in the account. You will need an adult to assist with setting up your account initially but once set up, it's yours to fill! You can deposit your hard-earned cash at a branch in your local shopping area or you may also be able to receive payment via internet banking, especially if your parents pay you directly from their account. And some things can also be paid for by transferring money through the internet or by going into the bank to withdraw your money, or by using a cash card at an ATM (automatic teller machine). Many banks or credit unions have special account set-ups for kids, so ask around to find the best one for you.

Partnerships with friends and/or family

You may prefer to create and work with a friend or your family so you can share the experience of making money. You can split everything (expenses and takings and input) 50/50 so you share everything, or depending on who does what you may split more to you with a 70/30 cut, as long as it represents fairly each partner's input. Remember, you want a win–win outcome for everyone. If you don't want to split everything, you may just pay someone a fee to assist you. Partnerships should be considered carefully and require honesty, trust and good communication. All concerned can earn more money than one person but only if they work well in a team or partnership.

Activities you can do with an adult

Breeding animals

To breed animals you need to mate two adults so that you can sell the offspring (babies) once they are ready to leave their parents. Dogs, cats, rabbits, mice, birds, fish and many other creatures are bred for reselling. This activity has very high responsibilities and must be done with an adult who has knowledge and experience. No animal must ever get distressed because you don't know what you're doing. However, when done properly, it can be very rewarding. You can use the support of breeder groups, pet shops and other personal breeders for information and for selling.

Restoring and selling furniture

While most kids can sand and paint, once taught the basics, this activity requires an adult to help lift, move, pick up and drop off the old and restored items. It can be a lot of fun visiting garage sales looking for rickety old chairs and tables that may also be antiques (older than 75 years, or 25 for cars) and fixing them up to keep or sell.

eBay

eBay is an internet-based trading center where all sorts of weird and wonderful and functional items are auctioned off. It has age limits requiring an adult to be the responsible trader. However, if you have a parent who loves to chase down a good bargain or you have things to sell, then there's no reason why you can't do all the hunting and groundwork; it's just that once you've found stuff, you can't do the actual trading without an adult.

Other ideas for older kids (12+)

Babysitting

All parents have different ideas about how old one needs to be to not need a babysitter, as they do about the age you need to be a babysitter! And once you reach "that" age then this is a great way to earn money. You have to be responsible and supervise your charges (the kid/s) at all times. The do's and don'ts will be set by the parents. You will need to know their whereabouts, their contact number as well as emergency numbers.

TOP TIP!

This can be a great time to catch up on your homework while your young "charge" is asleep.

House-sitting

House-sitting is mostly needed when people go away, so it sometimes requires staying overnight. It may just require visiting the premises every day to clear mail, water plants, feed any animals and maybe walk them. As soon as you're responsible enough to do these things then it's a great way to make money.

Shopping

Some people, if they are old or sick, or just too busy, may need assistance with their shopping. It might be grocery shopping at the local supermarket or even ordering it online for home delivery that's required. It may be clothes or gift shopping depending on what service you are confident you can offer. The most important thing for all shopping is to take a detailed list of what is needed so that you have less chance of getting the wrong things and then having to return them.

Errands

People often need small jobs done that you can do on a bike with a decent backpack or parcel rack, such as dropping off and picking up dry cleaning or prescriptions or delivering parcels. Is there a local shop that might benefit from offering a home delivery service that you could do after school? Ask around, it could be the butcher, the pharmacist or even the baker—but probably not the candlestick maker!

Useful tips and info

If you use the internet for any money transactions make sure the websites are authentic and secured. Don't access any sites from email links, only from the direct address typed into your browser. If you are unsure of the internet environment always have an adult assist you. Try not to carry large sums of money and never count it in public where you can be seen. Unfortunately, there are people who are desperate enough to rob you of your hard-earned money.

You might want to use a lock-up safety deposit box to keep your money in, but if it's portable and you use it at a market then make sure it stays out of others' sight (but not yours).

Teacher: "Nick, if you had $5 and you asked your father for $3 more, how many dollars would you have?"

Nick: "I would have five dollars..."

Teacher: "You don't know your arithmetic, Nick..."

Nick: "You don't know my father, sir."

My Savings Chart

Color in each box as you move closer to the $100 goal!

Goal:_____

Goal Achieved

$100   Date:_____   **$100! Congratulations!**

$90   Date:_____

$80   Date:_____

$70   Date:_____

$60   Date:_____

$50   Date:_____   **Halfway there!**

$40   Date:_____

$30   Date:_____

$20   Date:_____

$10   Date:_____

My Ideas

List or draw any new and inspired ideas!

Record-keeping

Record-keeping Book

To start your Record-keeping Book, simply fill in the following pages as you go (but first photocopy them so you have extra pages for later). If you're savvy with the Excel computer application you can even recreate them yourself, or use basic accounting software.

Basic income and expenses ledger

If you're not a numbers whiz then it might pay
(literally!) to ask an adult to help fill in this form. At
the end of each week or month, or even when you fill
up all the rows, add up your figures and subtract B
from A to give you C . . . and that will give you your
profit for that period of time. And of course hopefully
you've earned more than you've spent!

Track your time

Each time you start a new project or activity it's very
useful to keep a record of the time you spend. In that
way you can either charge for your time or factor it
in when you are costing goods to sell. If you spent
20 hours to find, fix or make something and can only
charge $20 for it then your time was probably not well
spent (unless you are happy to earn $1 per hour!).

Things to save for

It's very important to have goals. We all have things
that we want, so make a list of goals in the order that
you want to achieve them and keep the list somewhere
where you can see it—this will help you stick to your
savings plan.

THINGS TO SAVE FOR

No:	ITEM	1/4 saved by:	1/2 saved by:	3/4 saved by:	TARGET DATE	AMOUNT TO SAVE	GOT IT!
eg:	Bike	$30 Feb 1	$60 April 1	$90 June 1	August 1	$120.00	✔
1							
2							
3							
4							
5							
6							
7							
8							
9							
10							

TRACK YOUR EARNINGS

DATE	[A] INCOME	AMOUNT	DATE	[B] EXPENSES	AMOUNT
eg: June 30	Sold bike	$80	June 28	New tire and bell	$25.50

How to Make Money

[A] TOTALS $

[B] TOTALS $

With [A] Income TOTAL	$
Minus [B] Expenses TOTAL	- $
Equals [C] PROFIT	= $

Glossary

Glossary

Words often have more than one meaning. This list includes most of the more complex words used in this book, with their relevant definitions.

A

    A frame—stand-up sign that is hinged at the top, and from the side looks like a letter "A."

B

Barter—to negotiate a lower price than advertised or displayed.

Bookkeeping—the keeping of financial records.

Brand—the identity of a company or product.

Bucks—slang for currency notes.

C

Cash flow—amount of net cash generated by an investment or a business during a specific period.

Charge—to charge is to name a price.

Charges (1)—costs that you add to the price of an item.

Charges (2)—another name for kids who you are in charge of.

Contra—an equal exchange of goods or services.

Competitors—businesses that offer similar, or the same, goods/services as you do.

Currency—money, bills, and coins.

D

Deposit (1)—A transaction involving a transfer of funds to another party, like a bank for safekeeping.

Deposit (2)—To leave a deposit on something is to confirm your intention to buy it.

E

Economical—an approach that is worthwhile, time and money-wise.

F

Finances—the management of money and other assets.

Financial—pertaining to finances; dealings with money.

Flora—term to describe growing plants.

Forte—one's particular talent or suitability to something.

G

Goods—products for sale.

Greenback—the nickname for USA currency notes.

I

Interest—a percentage payment for the use of borrowed money.

L

Ledger—a record in which commercial accounts are recorded.

M

Marketing—the act of promoting one's business.

Milestones—smaller-spaced goals.

Mock—to create a sample of a product before it's produced.

Money—currency in bills and coins used to purchase, or received for goods and services.

P

Potential—the likely possibility of achieving something.

Product—goods that can be sold and bought.

Profit—the amount left over after your costs and expenses have been taken out of your takings or fees.

Promotion—to create a special offer, or advertise or publicize one's business.

Q

Quid pro quo—a Latin phrase meaning "favor for a favor."

R

Records (1)—financial figures kept in a ledger.

Records (2)—music on a vinyl disc.
Resellers—things that re-sell well.
RRP—recommended retail price.

S

Savings—after everything has been paid and you've taken out money you need to keep things going, you can call the left-over money your savings.
Services—an act or a variety of work done for others, especially for pay.
Skills—a developed talent or ability.
Spruiking—verbally selling your wares publicly.
Stock—a quantity of products held by a business.
Stock market—where the world's stocks are traded.
Strike—to grow roots from a plant cutting.

T

Testimonials—letters from satisfied customers.

V

Value—the worth placed on something.

W

Wares—another term for good or services.

My Ideas

List or draw any new and inspired ideas!

My Ideas

List or draw any new and inspired ideas!

My Ideas

List or draw any new and inspired ideas!

_____

_____

_____

_____

_____

_____

_____

_____

_____

_____

_____

My Ideas

List or draw any new and inspired ideas!

_____

_____

_____

_____

_____

_____

_____

_____

_____

_____

_____

My Ideas

List or draw any new and inspired ideas!

My Ideas

List or draw any new and inspired ideas!

_____

_____

_____

_____

_____

_____

_____

_____

_____

_____

_____

_____

My Ideas

List or draw any new and inspired ideas!

My Ideas

List or draw any new and inspired ideas!

My Ideas

List or draw any new and inspired ideas!

My Ideas

List or draw any new and inspired ideas!

My Ideas

List or draw any new and inspired ideas!

My Ideas

List or draw any new and inspired ideas!